Matt's Bike

Written by Sharon Wohl
Photographs by Celeste Schaadt

A Better Way of Learning
Creator of The Phonics Game™

A Better Way of Learning • www.phonicsgame.com

Matt likes his bike.
It is nine on the clock.
Matt has time to ride.

Mike helps Matt tune up and lube
his bike.
Mike can fix the tube and tire.
Mike tests the brakes.
The bike is fine.

Matt gets on the bike.
Matt rides fast.
Matt grins.
This is fun!

Matt jumps and skids on his bike.
He grips the brakes
and twists and spins the bike.

Yikes!
Matt takes a spill and scrapes
his leg.
Matt rests in the shade.
Ann helps with tape on Matt's leg.

Matt gets up. He is fine.
Matt thanks Ann, pets Duke and
gets back on his bike.
He rides to a hill.
Matt glides on the hill and smiles.

It is time to ride home and get lunch.
Matt had fun on his bike.
Matt likes to ride!

My little sister and brother
want to play too.

"I am a queen!"
says Ava.
Cash waves a magic wand.

I pull on a tutu.
Then I close my eyes.

I pretend I am a ballerina.
"Bravo!" cheers the crowd.

Next I put on
a white coat.

I pretend
I am a doctor.
I can make anyone
feel better!

Then I hear a screech.
"No, Cash!" yells Ava.
"Cooks do not use hoses!"

The hose lands on my doll.
"Hey!" I yell.

Cash starts to cry.

My mom enters the room.
"What is wrong?"
she asks.

"Cooks do not use hoses,"
Ava says.

"Firefighters do not
bother doctors,"
I say.

"Can a cook also be
a firefighter?"
my mom asks Ava.

Then she asks me,
"Can a doctor also be
a forgiving sister?"

"Everyone can be
more than one thing,"
my mom says.

"Just look at me!
I am a mom and a writer."

"Look!" Cash says.
He is wearing
a new costume.

Now he is
a superhero builder!

I put on a new costume too.
I dress up as
a mermaid teacher.

Ava dresses up as
a fairy artist.

"Playing dress-up
is the best thing
in the world!" Ava says.

"President Parker
does not agree,"
I say.

"It is the best
thing in the whole
universe!"

MAKING FASHION WAVES

Do you like playing dress-up like Parker? What are your favorite clothes and costumes to wear? Here are a few people who grew up to become famous fashion designers.

TRACY REESE is an American fashion designer who started her own clothing label in 1998. Many people have worn her designs, including Oprah Winfrey, Tracee Ellis Ross, Meghan Markle, and Michelle Obama! In 2019, Tracy created Hope for Flowers. The clothes in the Hope for Flowers line use sustainable materials that are better for the environment.

CHRISTOPHER JOHN ROGERS is an American fashion designer. Although he's still at the beginning of his career, he has already won many major awards! He also designed the outfit Vice President Kamala Harris wore on Inauguration Day when she was sworn in as the first Black American, the first South Asian American, and the first woman vice president of the United States of America.

STELLA JEAN (say: JOHN) was born in Rome, Italy. She was a model before becoming a fashion designer. Stella tried out twice for a famous Italian fashion contest, but she was rejected both times. She didn't give up, though. On her third try, she won second place. Many of Stella's designs are inspired by her Haitian and Italian background.

If you could design new clothes or accessories, what would they look like? Try drawing your ideas in a sketchbook!